What Was It Like Growing Up in the 70s?

A Journal to Revisit and Share the Groovy 70s

~ Riya Aarini ~

This book belongs to '70s kid

Contents

Welcome to Your '70s History!

The 1970s was a largely uncomplicated decade in which to grow up. Kids spent free time outside, roaming the neighborhoods until dark without causing the least bit of parental worry. Friendships blossomed upon talking for hours in person and sharing life experiences.

Despite limited options during the decade, a sense of societal happiness proliferated. People in the '70s performed tasks independent of technology, yet still got things done. On-demand availability was unheard of, giving films and purchases a greater specialness.

Via this journal, return to an era of riveting political scandals and war—as well as electrifying music, distinct fashion, and some of the most influential movies in history, from "Star Wars" to "Jaws." The '70s was one hip decade that remains close to the hearts of '70s kids!

Birthdays

Common '70s party venues included the backyard, family home, and party room at fast-food restaurants.

Where did you celebrate your birthdays?

List five groovy birthday gifts you received in the '70s.

_____

_____

_____

_____

_____

Did you enjoy homemade birthday cakes or cakes from the bakery? If homemade, who baked them?

Did you bring treats, like cupcakes, for your entire class on your birthday?

What party games did your guests play?

Did you throw birthday slumber parties? If so, describe a memorable one.

School

What was your favorite class?

How did you learn to type? On an electric or manual typewriter?

Did you pass handwritten notes in class?

Describe one of the funniest or most embarrassing.

Describe a time a teacher intercepted and read the note out loud.

How well did you perfect the origami-like folding?

What foods did school lunches consist of?

How much did a small carton of milk or chocolate milk cost?

Were you ever sent to detention? If so, why?

Cursive

If you learned cursive in school, do you now feel privileged to be a part of one of the last generations to read and write cursive?

Yearbooks

Did you sign classmates' elementary, junior high, or high school yearbooks?

Do you recall any memorable messages, inside jokes, or well-wishes?

How important was it to you to autograph yearbooks or have yours autographed?

Extracurricular Activities

What extracurricular activities did you participate in?

If you were in the school band, what instrument did you play?

If you were athletic, what sports did you play?

If you served on the school newspaper, what was your role?

Graduation

How did it feel to graduate elementary school, middle school, or high school in the '70s?

Describe your graduation ceremony, if your school had one.

What are your best memories of graduation?

Friends

Friendships in the '70s exuded a genuine quality, as they formed over multiple face-to-face interactions or, at times, instantly. Bonds between youth grew strong with regular play and communication.

Did you have a few or many friends growing up in the '70s?

How did you bond with your childhood friends? Movies, music, hobbies?

Did you talk on a landline with friends? Recount any annoyance with the length of the phone cord.

How long did phone conversations last?

Did you host or attend sleepovers? What were they like?

Was camp a part of your childhood? Describe the best and worst of camp.

Did you knock on friends' doors to ask if they could come out and play?

Do you feel you had the freedom to be a kid in the '70s?

How would you describe the quality of friendships in the '70s? Stronger, more personal?

Friendship Bracelets

Friendship bracelets first gained traction in the United States during the '70s. The woven bracelets symbolized peace and love—ideals embraced by the era's hippies.

Did you weave friendship bracelets with colorful thread?

Did you trade friendship bracelets at camp, school, elsewhere?

How many friendship bracelets did you wear at a time on your wrists?

Did you ever take them off? How tattered did they get?

Were friendship bracelets a status symbol of your '70s childhood?

Fashion

Fashion in the '70s included bellbottoms, high-waisted jeans, round sunglasses, and platform shoes. The mood ring craze took the decade by storm before fading in popularity.

What '70s fashion trend did you try and like?

What '70s fashion trend did you try and dislike?

Describe whether the hippie movement or bohemian culture influenced your fashion choices.

Did you wear tie-dye shirts? If so, did you dye them yourself?

Name a '70s accessory you wouldn't leave home without.

Did you adorn yourself with puka shell necklaces in the '70s?

Did you wear mood rings? If so, did the changing colors accurately reflect your mood?

Hair

Hairdos in the '70s varied dramatically, from straight styles to bold disco curls and famed shag cuts.

How did you style your hair in the '70s?

Did you wear your hair naturally, in long braids, loose waves, or with a side or center part?

Did you adopt the feathered look trending in the '70s?

How did you adorn your hair? Headbands, flower crowns?

Holidays

Valentine's Day

How did you celebrate the day of love in the '70s?

Did you pass out handmade Valentine's Day cards to classmates?

Did you receive Valentine's Day cards from classmates? If so, do you still have them, perhaps tucked away in a box in the attic?

Did you decorate a Valentine's Day box for class to collect cards and candy?

Did you munch on Valentine's Day treats? If so, which ones?

July the Fourth

How did you celebrate Independence Day in the '70s?

Did you light sparklers or go big with fireworks?

Did you watch or join the Fourth of July parades? Describe the feelings they inspired.

Halloween

List three favorite Halloween costumes you wore in the '70s.

_____

_____

_____

Did you wear store-bought or handmade costumes? If homemade, who sewed them?

Did you trick-or-treat? What did you use to collect candy: plastic bucket, paper bag, pillow case?

What did you think about homes that gave out king-size candy bars?

What was your favorite Halloween candy? What was your least favorite?

Did you trade candy with fellow trick-or-treaters?

Did your parents impose a tax on your Halloween candy?

List one unusual thing you received while trick-or-treating.

How late did you stay out freely roaming the streets on Halloween night?

Did you play Ouija boards and Bloody Mary?

Did you watch Halloween specials on TV? If so, which ones?

Did you play Halloween pranks on unsuspecting adults? If so, describe one!

How magical was Halloween in the '70s?

Politics

Vietnam War

How did the Vietnam War impact your childhood, if at all?

Did the barrage of political turmoil and violence broadcasted on the news affect you?

Watergate

Did your family hold conversations about Watergate, the event dominating the political landscape from 1972 to 1974?

How much trust did you place in US President Richard Nixon during the Watergate scandal?

Did you attend political protests?

Cold War

Did your school run drills to prepare for a possible nuclear attack?

Did your family discuss the possibility of nuclear war?

What mark did the Cold War leave on you, if any?

Books

List five books you enjoyed reading in the '70s.

_____

_____

_____

_____

_____

Name your favorite childhood book series.

Popular authors included Shel Silverstein, Judy Blume, and Roald Dahl.

Who was your favorite author?

Did you perform extra chores to earn money to buy books?

How often did you visit the library to check out books?

Did you think the books, such as Walter Farley's "The Black Stallion," were better than the film adaptations?

News

Newspapers

Did your family buy newspapers from the newsstand or subscribe to home deliveries?

If so, what sections did you read? Comics, others?

Magazines

What favorite '70s magazines did you subscribe to or buy individually?

Radio

Did you listen to AM radio to hear the news?

Board Games

Board games entertained '70s youth at home. Classic games played during the decade included Boggle, Clue, Operation, and Monopoly.

What board games did you play in the '70s?

With whom did you play board games?

Did your family hold family game nights?

Movies

Popular '70s movies included
1971: "Willy Wonka & the Chocolate Factory"
1975: "Jaws"
1977: "Star Wars"

Name your three favorite '70s movies.

_____

_____

_____

Where did you watch movies? At the movie theater, home?

Did you consider old movies broadcasted on television to be major events, since they aired once annually?

What movie best described the '70s?

Television

More '70s households started to make the shift to color televisions, which elevated the TV viewing experience to new heights.

List your three favorite television sitcoms or cartoons.

_____

_____

_____

Did you rush home after school to watch TV? If so, which shows?

Did you refer to the "TV Guide" to catch shows?

How many channels did your '70s television have?

How did you adjust the television antenna?

How did you change the channels?

Was your TV black and white or color?

If you rewatched '70s TV shows on a color TV in later years, did the color leave you spellbound?

Flashes from the '70s Past

Flashes from the '70s Past

Conversations

Did you enjoy the face-to-face conversations of the '70s?

Did a sense of casualness permeate the '70s?

Did you feel more connected to people (the music store clerk, strangers on the bus, or even friends) in the '70s?

Did you pepper your speech with popular '70s slang?

Do you catch yourself still using these words today?

Music

Music in the '70s ranged from glam rock to disco. Youth developed eclectic musical tastes upon listening to the era's diverse range of music.

What were your favorite '70s music genres?

Which music artists or bands did you enjoy most?

List three songs you replayed over and over.

_____

_____

_____

Did you listen to the radio? Did it expose you to a greater variety of music?

Did you ever call up the radio station and ask the DJ to play a song you wanted to hear?

What '70s song described you as a youth?

Vinyl Records

Did you visit the record stores?

Name three vinyl records you bought in the '70s.

_____

_____

_____

Did you own a record player?

Did you belong to a record club to obtain deals on records?

Did you own a record collection? What artists were a part of your collection?

Did you ever accidentally scratch a record? How did your parents react?

Mixtapes

Did you create your own mixtapes?

Did you make mixtapes for friends?

Considering the time and effort it took to create mixtapes, what significance did they hold for you?

Elvis Presley

What did you think of Elvis Presley's music or showmanship?

How did you react to Elvis's untimely death on August 16, 1977?

The Beatles

Did your parents play Beatles music?

Did the Beatles influence your youth? If so, in what ways?

How did you feel when the Beatles disbanded in 1970?

Staying Connected

Rotary Phones

Did you make calls on a rotary phone?

How long did it take to dial on a rotary phone?

Did you memorize friends' phone numbers? If so, how many could you remember?

Did you carry around a mini planner with friends' phone numbers scribbled in it?

How did you coordinate phone calls, since people had to be by the phone to receive them?

Without the convenience of smartphones, how did you react when friends didn't show up for planned get-togethers?

Pay Phones

Did you carry around nickels and dimes in case you needed to use a pay phone?

How much did you rely on pay phones?

Did you ever call collect? Give an example of a time you asked the operator to make a collect call.

Did you ever find coins in the coin return? How thrilled did you feel?

Phone Books

How often did you use the phone book? Whose numbers did you look up?

Did your family pay the phone book company to keep your number unlisted?

Did you comb through the phone book, looking for people with the same name as you?

Did you ever prank call someone using a number listed in the phone book? Describe the prank!

Answering Machines

Did your family use an answering machine?

How many messages did your answering machine hold?

What was one of the funniest answering machine messages you'd heard?

Letters

Did you write letters on decorative stationery?

Did you receive any letters that became your favorites?

Do you still have these letters, like in a keepsake box?

Greeting Cards

What was one of the most memorable greeting cards you received in the '70s?

Did you give homemade greeting cards? If so, describe one and the recipient's reaction.

Prom

Did you go to prom? If so, describe your formalwear.

If your prom had a theme, what was it?

Describe the fun prom atmosphere, such as glittery disco balls, lava lamps, or beaded curtains.

Did you take the traditional prom photo? Would you describe it as cringeworthy or memorable? What made it so?

What was your prom song?

Was it performed by a live band?

What lasting memories did prom celebrations create?

Dating

If you dated, where did you go on dates? Friends' gatherings, bowling alley, the mall?

Did your date ask your parents for permission before taking you out?

How did you connect with dates? Phone conversations, letters, hanging out?

Did dating in the '70s require more effort?

Do you feel dating was more sincere in the '70s, since it was based on face-to-face interactions?

Video Games

Did you play video games in the '70s? If so, on a home console or at the arcade?

If you visited the arcade, describe the experience.

List your top three video games from the '70s.

_____

_____

_____

Did you prefer spending time playing outdoors over playing video games?

Food

Buffet-style restaurants grew to be a cultural phenomenon during the '70s, due to their affordable dining options and wide variety of dishes.

Did your family dine at all-you-can-eat buffets?

What was your favorite buffet restaurant?

What menu item did you enjoy most?

As a kid, did you eat free at the buffets? How cool was that?

What was your favorite homecooked meal?

Name your favorite '70s snacks.

Celebrities

Who were your favorite '70s celebrities in music, movies, or sports?

What did you admire about them?

Did you get to meet any of them in person? If so, where?

Leisure Activities

'70s kids stayed active, riding their bikes, roller skating, fishing, camping, or exploring the woods until dark.

What physical activities did you participate in during the '70s?

Summer

Summer was a time for catching frogs at the creek, swinging on ropes, water balloon fights, riding mini bikes, watching cartoons on Saturday mornings, and climbing trees.

Summer Vacations

What did you do during the never-ending summer vacations?

Family Vacations

Did your family vacation when school was out for the summer?

Describe one memorable family vacation spot.

If you took road trips with family, what car games did you play?

Did your family consult paper maps during road trips?

Did the family car have A/C?

Where did you stop for food during road trips?

What memories did family road trips create?

Bedroom

What posters hung on your '70s bedroom wall?

Did a lava lamp light up your bedroom with vibrant neon colors? If so, what inspired you to add it to your bedroom?

Did shag carpeting line your bedroom floor? If so, what was your opinion of it?

Hobbies

What hobbies did you enjoy in the '70s?

Did you have any prize collections, like baseball cards, stamps, or coins?

Malls

How important was the mall to your '70s childhood? A place for a first job, first date?

How often did you hang out at the mall with friends?

Did you explore malls to discover the latest fashion trends or the newest in music?

What did you find appealing about strolling around the sea of stores, kiosks, arcades, movie theaters, and eateries?

Jobs

Common jobs for '70s kids included babysitting, newspaper delivery, and lawn mowing.

If you worked in the '70s, what jobs did you hold?

How much did you earn?

What did you spend your earnings on?

Lemonade Stands

Did you operate a lemonade stand?

If so, how much did you charge per cup?

Did you turn a profit?

How did you advertise? Posterboard signs, word-of-mouth?

Intangibles

What was your biggest takeaway of the decade?

Did '70s culture give you any aha moments? If so, what was one of them?

What goals did you set for yourself in the '70s? Did you achieve them?

Describe one major accomplishment you are most proud of.

Who was your '70s hero, real or imagined? Why did you look up to them?

In the '70s, who did you want to be, professionally or personally, when you grew up?

What about the '70s are you most grateful for?

Growing up in the '70s, what did you most want to change about the world?

What aspects of the '70s excited you?

What was an average day like in the '70s?

Describe your best, most unforgettable day.

Describe your worst, most forgettable day.

What values did you hold in the '70s?

What was the biggest risk you took in the '70s?

What would have made the '70s better than it was?

What about the '70s do you wish continued to the present day?

What was it like to celebrate New Year's Eve in 1979?

Sum up the '70s in one word.

_____

More Flashes from the '70s Past

More Flashes from the '70s Past

Long Live the '70s!

A nswering these prompts might've returned you to carefree times, even if for a splendid moment. By sharing the completed journal, your loved ones gain insights into a slice of the irreplicable '70s culture that you are privileged to have been an important part of. That's far out!

Books in the
What Was It Like series

What Was It Like Growing Up in the 80s?
A Journal to Revisit and Share the Totally Awesome 80s

What Was It Like During Christmas in the 80s?
A Journal to Revisit and Share the 80s Holiday Spirit

What Was It Like Growing Up in the 90s?
A Journal to Revisit and Share the Rad 90s

What Was It Like During Christmas in the 90s?
A Journal to Revisit and Share the 90s Holiday Vibe

What Was It Like Marrying in the 80s?
A Journal (for Her) to Revisit and Share 80s Wedding Bliss

What Was It Like Marrying in the 90s?
A Journal (for Her) to Revisit and Share 90s Wedding
Magic

www.ingramcontent.com/pod-product-compliance
Lightning Source LLC
Chambersburg PA
CBHW051314120626
46547CB00015B/2228